Pebble® Plus

Investigate the Seasons

Let's Look at Winter

Revised Edition

by Sarah L. Schuette

CAPSTONE PRESS
a capstone imprint

Pebble Plus is published by Capstone Press,
1710 Roe Crest Drive, North Mankato, Minnesota 56003
www.capstonepub.com

Library of Congress Cataloging-in-Publication Data
is available on the Library of Congress website.

ISBN 978-1-5435-0845-1 (library binding)
ISBN 978-1-5435-0873-4 (paperback)
ISBN 978-1-5435-0877-2 (ebook pdf)

Editorial Credits
Sarah Bennett, designer; Tracy Cummins, media researcher,
Laura Manthe, production specialist

Photo Credits
Shutterstock: Africa Studio, 5, Bakusova, 19, Dieter Hawlan, 1,
FotoRequest, Cover, Jeff Thrower, 17, Jim Cumming, 13, Khomulo Anna,
3, Liubou Yasiukovich, Cover Design Element, Marina Zezelina, 9,
Ondrej Prosicky, 15, Peter Wey, 21, SnvvSnvvSnvv, 7, tim elliott, 11

Note to Parents and Teachers

The Investigate the Seasons set supports national science standards
related to weather and life science. This book describes and illustrates
the season of winter. The images support early readers in understanding
the text. The repetition of words and phrases helps early readers learn
new words. This book also introduces early readers to subject-specific
vocabulary words, which are defined in the Glossary section. Early
readers may need assistance to read some words and to use the Table
of Contents, Glossary, Read More, Internet Sites, Critical Thinking
Questions, and Index sections of the book.

Printed in the United States   5594

Table of Contents

It's Winter!

How do you know it's winter?

The temperature is cold.

The ground hardens.

Water freezes.

When snow falls,

it covers everything.

The sun rises later
in the morning.
Winter days are
the shortest of the year.

9

Animals in Winter

What do animals do

in winter?

Deer search for food

under the snow.

Some brown rabbits turn white.

Now their fur blends in

with the snow.

Owls sit in snowy trees.

They stay

for the whole winter.

Some birds migrate.

Plants in Winter

What happens

to plants in winter?

They do not grow.

Many plants look bare

and brown.

Evergreen trees stay green.
They keep their needles
all year round.

What's Next?

The temperature gets warmer.

Winter is over.

What season is next?

Glossary

bare—not covered

evergreen—a tree or bush that has green needles all year long

freeze—to become solid or icy at a very low temperature

migrate—to move from one place to another when seasons change

needle—a sharp, green leaf on an evergreen tree

season—one of the four parts of the year; winter, spring, summer, and fall are seasons

temperature—the measure of how hot or cold something is

Read More

Phillips, Dee. *Snowshoe Hare.* Arctic Animals. New York: Bearport Publishing, 2015.

Rustad, Martha E. H. *All About Animals in Winter.* Celebrate Winter. North Mankato, Minn.: Capstone Press, 2016.

Ward, Jennifer. *What Will Grow?* New York: Bloomsbury, 2017.

Internet Sites

Use FactHound to find Internet sites related to this book.

Visit *www.facthound.com*

Just type **9781543508451** and go.

 Check out projects, games and lots more at
www.capstonekids.com

Critical Thinking Questions

1. How does white fur help some rabbits in winter?

2. What happens to the days in winter?

3. Describe what you like to do in winter.

Index